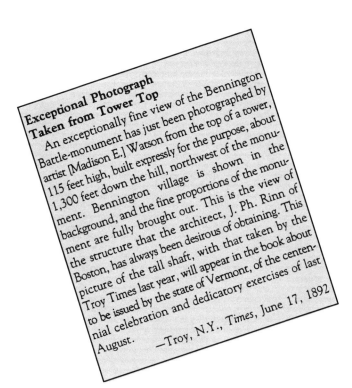

Bennington's Battle Monum

M assive and Lofty

This early formal portrait of the Bennington Battle Monument, probably taken by photographer Madison E. Watson, was used as the frontispiece of the first official book about the Bennington Monument, published in 1892. The book contained the full text of all addresses and documents relating to the mammoth double celebration in 1891 when the monument was dedicated and Vermont also marked its 100th anniversary as a state.

ent:

An illustrated interpretive history
by Tyler Resch
with a picture essay by Julius Rosenwald

Beech Seal Press
Bennington, Vermont

Acknowledgments

The principal narrative of this book was adapted from an article published in *Vermont Life* magazine in the summer of 1988 on the centennial of the construction of the Bennington Battle Monument.

The endpapers, front and back, are portions of a birdseye view of the community drawn in 1887, before aviation existed to confirm what that view might actually look like. The year 1887 was also when the monument's cornerstone was laid; hence it was confidently premature to include the completed monument in the scene.

Unless otherwise credited, older photographs are from the collection of Images from the Past, Bennington, Vermont. Modern photographs were taken by the author, except for those taken from the capstone by the intrepid Julius Rosenwald. Sketches of alternative monument designs are by Karen Kane, from a variety of sources. Gratitude is expressed to the Bennington Museum for the Chambers design on page 54. The map of the monument site and grounds is by Ellen K. Viereck.

ISBN 1-884592-00-7

Beech Seal Press
P.O. Box 4422
Bennington, Vermont 05201
Tordis Ilg Isselhardt and Tyler Resch, partners.

Ordering information: for prepaid copies send $9.95 per book plus $2.50 for shipping and handling (plus .50 for each additional book) to Beech Seal Press, P.O. Box 4422, Bennington, Vt. 05201. Phone and fax: 802 442-3204. Vermont residents add 5% sales tax to cost of book. Please allow two to three weeks for delivery. Include name and street address for proper delivery.

View from the capstone, December 1, 1889

This grand view of the nearly treeless village of Bennington Centre (today known as Old Bennington) could only be taken after the Battle Monument's pyramid-shaped capstone had been cemented into place in November 1889. The pre-aviation "aerial" photograph proved to be memorably provocative to the public. To take it, photographer Madison E. Watson ascended to the summit in a basket designed for hauling cement.

Hiland Hall won the dispute over the monument's design after his 90th birthday in July 1885. He died before the cornerstone was laid in 1887.

Since it was built in the late 1880s, the "massive and lofty" Bennington Battle Monument has dominated the landscape for many miles around southwestern Vermont. The monument forms a companion and visual counterpoint to Mount Anthony, the 2,300-foot Taconic mountain which rises to its south and which also towers above the territory.

Indeed, both the mountain and the monument are ingrained in the consciousness of the Bennington community. These images are reiterated daily—in the logo of the town's newspaper, the *Bennington Banner*, in the names of other local businesses such as Monument Electric, Monument Roofing, or Mount Anthony Country Club, and even the regional public high school, Mount Anthony Union.

To those who come upon it for the first time, the Bennington Battle

1

The First Contribution

At a well attended meeting of the Directors of the Historical Society, on Monday evening, the following resolution was passed. The meeting was adjourned till Friday evening, which should also be well attended:

"Resolved, That the Board of Directors of the Bennington Historical Society hereby express the thanks of this society to Mrs. Ominda Gerry, for her contribution of $100 —the first contribution made to the proposed Bennington Battle Monument; and they would take the liberty of suggesting that in this expression of thanks, they not only manifest the gratitude of this society, but of every citizen of Bennington and Vermont as well."

—*Bennington Banner*, Oct. 5, 1876

Congressman's Oration
At Cornerstone Rites

Let it rise majestic here, girt by these grand mountains, commanding views of unmatched natural beauty and overlooking graves of the heroic dead. And so may it stand, a mute but eloquent witness and memorial to all coming generations of the Battle of Bennington and of the valor and virtue of the men who crowned the day, whose anniversary we celebrate, with glorious victory.

—*From the oration of Congressman John W. Stewart of Middlebury at "Bennington's Great Day of Universal Patriotism," the laying of the cornerstone of the monument*
August 16, 1887.

This diorama depicting the second engagement of the Battle of Bennington, August 16, 1777, constructed by Paul V. Winters in 1964, is found just inside the monument's entrance.

Monument looms up as unexpectedly gigantic. Had it not been for the visionary tenacity of one influential citizen, this monumental obelisque would have been much less impressive, a structure tucked away on a knoll and viewed almost by accident, the way many Civil War markers and monuments are often designed and located.

Bennington's monument towers over the countryside on such a grand scale because of the determination of Hiland Hall, Vermont's pre-eminent nineteenth-century historian, who had been a U.S. congressman, governor and supreme court justice, and who also served his nation in the pioneering role of federal land commissioner to California in the early 1850s. Hall chose to make the final struggle of his long life a contest to achieve a design for the Bennington Battle Monument that would be—to use his words—truly monumental, massive, and lofty.

The evidence of Hall's success stands as a stone tower, 306 feet tall, including the bronze star at its peak. By the time it was completed in 1889, the dolomite monument had cost about $112,000 (in an era when a working person's house could be built for $1,000). It is twice as tall as the Saratoga Battle Monument, which marks the more-important battle that put an end to the British "Gentleman Johnny" Burgoyne's military campaign of 1777. Though Bennington's monument is some 250 feet shorter than the Washington Monument, its loftiness sometimes appears even greater than the Washington (which is 555 feet high) because the Bennington monument is already located on a high promontory, itself 873 feet above sea level. If one measures monuments

Major General John Stark of New Hampshire, who commanded patriot forces, became one of several heroes of the Battle of Bennington. His wife Molly stayed home but was immortalized by Stark's pre-battle oratory: "There go the Redcoats, boys. They are ours, or tonight Molly Stark sleeps a widow."

3

"Monument key kept here" proclaimed an early sign at the caretaker's house on Monument Circle. The cost of a visit was 10 cents; the honor system prevailed.

Enduring fame
for architect Rinn

The building committee of the battle monument report progress. During the week a contractor, Wm. H. Ward of Lowell, Mass., has been here and negotiations are well advanced toward the completion of a contract very favorable to the association. The monument is to be 300 feet high and of the design adopted nearly two years ago. We have seen the working plans and from all appearances there will be no delay when the work commences. If the promise of this design is realized, when the monument is finally completed, Mr. Rinn will have gained an enduring fame, and we see no reason why the reality shall not fulfill the expectation of the Sixteenth of August this year.
—*Bennington Banner*, May 19, 1887.

Stonework Commences

The labor of putting in the foundation of the Battle Monument is well begun. Solid rock has been reached at a depth of about fifteen feet and the stone work is commenced. The Fillmore quarry proves to contain excellent building stone and the Lyman quarry exceeds expectations in the quality of the stock quarried. The work of getting out

starting at sea level, then Bennington's is far higher than the Washington Monument.

The Bennington monument was built to commemorate the Battle of Bennington of August 16, 1777, when northern New England's settlers proved that they could coalesce around an independent, even nationalistic, fighting spirit. The three-hour battle short-circuited a British strategy that would have isolated New England from the other colonies. It stung the British and their German mercenaries under the command of General Burgoyne. It repaid the British for the licking they inflicted on a patriot rear-guard force a few weeks earlier at the Battle of Hubbardton, the only Revolutionary War military engagement fought on Vermont soil. And the Battle of Bennington rallied the American forces who, two months later, accepted Burgoyne's surrender after the pivotal dual battles near Saratoga. The British loss at Saratoga,

A U.S. Geological Survey benchmark, showing 873 feet above sea level, is embedded in stone next to monument's entrance.

Below, one of many early panoramic views of downtown Bennington shows monument in distance. In foreground are North Street shops, circa 1895. The spire is that of St. Francis de Sales Church on West Main Street; visible just to its left is the Old First Church.

The monument grew just so far without scaffolding, as these photographs demonstrate. The derrick that leveraged up the stones moved from a base on the ground to the structure's center. Temporary rail line that hauled the material is seen in photo above, at left.

Watson,

BENNINGTON, VT

The obelisque kept growing ever taller throughout 1888 and 1889. The picture above, taken by photographer Madison E. Watson, includes only suggestions of both the railroad track and the derrick. At left: about three-quarters complete and still rising.

7

The capstone-hoisting effort of November 1889 halted the heavy block halfway up for the benefit of several photographers present, whose equipment did not lend itself to "action." The caption "Capstone ready to swing into place" was pasted onto the glass negative of this photo.

in turn, brought in the French on the side of the embryonic American nation.

Historians therefore often call the Battle of Bennington "the turning point of the turning point" of the American Revolution. It was the first action of a surprisingly successful one-two punch against an invading army. Proclaiming that American independence was "leveraged" at Bennington would be accurate. While the actual fighting took place a few miles west of Bennington, in Walloomsac, New York, the American victory prevented Burgoyne's troops from seizing supplies—corn, flour, horses, cattle—in a storehouse on the hill where the monument now stands. And thus the battle has taken on the name of Burgoyne's objective and not that of the location of the combat itself.

To Vermonters of all eras, the battle was one of their finest hours. Yet back in the 1870s, as the 100th anniversary of the battle approached, there had been no tangible memorial built to mark this illustrious achievement. Hiland Hall, who had served two one-

Gloriously framed by elms, a tree rarely seen in such abundance today, a family outing poses, circa 1895, with the seemingly omnipresent monument in the background.

"dimension" material has not yet been reached.

Meantime preparations for the cornerstone laying the Sixteenth of August are well under weigh (sic). Col. George W. Hooker is to be chief marshal, the militia are to encamp here from the 10th to the 18th of that month and no doubt that full programme will be indicated soon. It will be an occasion worthy the cause and the state, but the greater celebration is reserved for the completion of the monument two years later.

—*Bennington Banner*, June 23, 1887

Foundation Stone Laid

Yesterday afternoon at 4 o'clock, the first stone was laid in the foundation of the Battle Monument, in the presence of a number of our people, among whom we notice Maj. A. B. Valentine, John T. Shurtleff, Benj. R. Sears, Col. Olin Scott, John V. Hall, C. E. Hoadley; and also several ladies. The foundation begins from ten to fifteen feet below the surface and after something of an excavation in the surface rock. The solid bed-rock is not flat, but lies in drifts towards the north-east, making the best kind of a foundation for such a structure.

The leveling up of the bottom is completed, and none of it can be moved unless the whole top of

Old Bennington Village, site of the town's first settlement, in 1761, took on a new look with completion of the monument. The white block in center is the base for a statue of the snarling catamount and also marks the site, at right, of the Green Mountain Boys' "Catamount Tavern," which burned in 1871.

10

year terms as governor between 1858 and 1860, and who had published an impressive 500-page *Early History of Vermont* in 1868, led the effort to remedy the situation. He believed that no ordinary marker or monument would be adequate to the important task, a tribute to such an extraordinary event that had taken place here.

A native of North Bennington, born in 1795, Hall was an honorable politician who was meticulous in his approach to public issues, and a prolific writer and historian. As he neared 90 years of age he became a vigorous champion for the cause of appropriately fashioning the monument by which the Battle of Bennington would always be remembered.

After 1865 Hall and his wife Dolly lived in an apartment in the Victorian North Bennington mansion built by their son-in-law, Trenor W. Park, who had made a fortune as a lawyer in Gold Rush-rich California. From his

Bennington Village, which did not exist in 1777, grew up in the intervening century, gaining strongly during the 1840s when it began to outpopulate "Bennington Centre" up on the hill. This view from the lower village's aptly named Grandview Street is punctuated by the monument along the western horizon.

11

While under construction, the monument became a popular background for the relatively new art of photography. In this Watson photo, taken in 1888, the driver of the carriage is identified only as "Dr. Burgess." The identity of the others, including the gentleman at right wielding a rake, is not known.

the hill slides off, which of course is a physical impossibility. This first stone was from the Lyman quarry, was $7\frac{1}{2} \times 4 \times 2$ feet in dimensions, and weighed four tons. The walls below the surface of the ground are nine feet thick and are to be laid with the exact regularity that will be apparent when the monument rises above the ground.

There are about 25 men employed now, about the site, exclusive of the teamsters and the quarrymen. The work will progress rapidly. Some friction has occurred on account of a proposed railroad track to the Lyman quarry from the site, and we are told that this has been arranged.

—*Bennington Banner*, June 30, 1887

Art Critic Lauds
Design Simplicity

Lyman H. Weeks, a well-known art critic of Boston, has furnished the following description of the foundation and monument:

"You cannot fail to be impressed with the simplicity of the structure. There has been no straining for after effect, no attempt at meretricious ornament. The architect has held himself firmly and consistently to the idea of making a structure that

home in what is now known as the Park-McCullough House, Hall devoted the last twenty years of his life to history. As the second president of the Vermont Historical Society, he took part in statewide research projects during an era when the railroads gave free tickets to VHS members for their official travels. Hall's *Early History* drums a consistent beat, ardently defending the hard-working settlers of the New Hampshire Grants while castigating the treacherous Yorkers who held designs on this important but disputed territory between the Connecticut and Hudson rivers.

In 1875 Hall became the founding president of the Bennington Historical Society. Chief among the group's ambitious goals was the construction of a monument to the famous local battle. The society's 1877 celebration combined commemoration of the battle with the one hundredth anniversary of Vermont's declaration of independence (which formally took place in Windsor) and there were lengthy parades and patriotic speeches by local and state dignitaries. President Rutherford B. Hayes, along with members of his cabinet, came to Bennington to speak.

A 1913 postcard view, taken from partway up Mt. Anthony, shows the monument against a background of the Green Mountain Range and a landscape of open fields. At right is the Old First Church, with the old Mt. Anthony Seminary in front of it.

would be beautiful and impressive in itself alone. There are no balconies, no conspicuous outlooks; in fact, nothing of features of that character which would give the structure the air of an observatory. It is a memorial shaft, not an observatory, that the architect has devised and as such it will forever stand, grand in its simplicity, beautiful in its airy gracefulness and full of dignity and repose."
—*Bennington Reformer*, August 19, 1887

'Rugged Sentinel' Will Boost Business

. . . [T]he Bennington Battle monument . . . is decidedly the most magnificent structure and far-reaching in importance of anything ever erected in town. It is not only a good thing to have, but it will carry the name of our town down to far distant ages. Aside from the sentimental and educational phase of this event, we are of the opinion that our people have hardly yet begun to realize what the monument finished will do for the town. An imposing structure, second only to the Washington monument in height, it will be visited by thousands in summer, and will have a great tendency to call city people's attention to the great advantages of our town as a resort. The scenery hereabouts is grand, and the climate is invigorating. That rugged sentinel, commemorative of the hardy yeomanry who "fought at Bennington" will become the greatest advertisement of our mountains and valleys, our peaceful homes and happy firesides. Nothing to equal it in this capacity could have been devised. And at the same time we are perpetuating a noble history. . .
—*Bennington Banner*, January 5, 1888

Monument Rises to 40 Feet

Architect Rinn was in town Wednesday to inspect the progress of the battle monument. That structure has now attained a height of about forty feet."
—*Bennington Banner*, June 1, 1888

'Pointing Up' Proceeds Throughout the Winter

It was a mistake to roof in and quit work on the battle monument last fall, since many feet might have been added to its height during this glorious

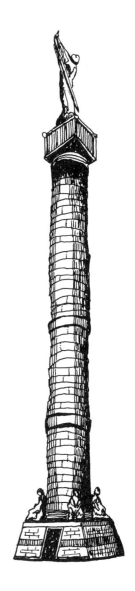

An early design by architect J. Phillipp Rinn and Vermont sculptor Truman D. Bartlett. It was publicized as early as 1877 in Leslie's Illustrated Newspaper as a fundraising enticement. It would have been only 100 feet high.

14

On the Road to Battle Monument,
Bennington, Vermont. *albany*

Different postcard views of the monument number in the hundreds and still sell by the thousands. Among the more picturesque were those of the old red covered bridge, above. The bridge burned in 1947 and was located on a road, no longer in use, that led north from the monument. In center is a 1905 card featuring a melange of local historic sites. At bottom, a hand-tinted view of the State Arms House, demolished to make way for the park that surrounds the monument.

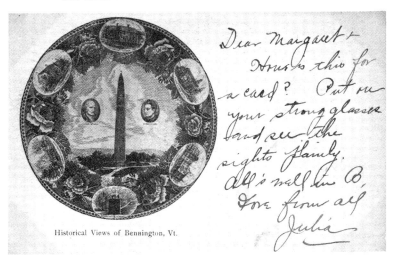

Historical Views of Bennington, Vt.

Dear Margaret —
How is this for a card? Put on your strong glasses and see the sights plainly. All's well in B. Love from all Julia

No. 11402, State Arms, Bennington, Vt.

15

BATTLE GROUND, BENNINGTON.

A 19th-century steel engraving of the placid field in Walloomsac, N.Y., where the Bennington Battle took ⸢ *Below, the rejected "artistic" design of Professor John* ⸢ *Weir of Yale University.*

winter. But stone cutting progresses rapidly and now workmen are engaged in "pointing" up the interior and doing other work that would naturally be deferred till spring.

In quarrying stone in the Fillmore quarry for the battle monument, marble of good quality has been struck. This circumstance is of great value to the owner and to the town. This may yet be the center of the marble business of the state.
—*Bennington Banner*, January 18, 1889

Bennington Moves Up
On Scale of Importance

Bennington has moved up one more degree in the scale of importance in being chosen by several great railroad corporations as a summer-excursion point . . . The headquarters for excursionists will be in the beautiful grove at the Vermont soldiers' home . . . An ample and tasteful dancing pavilion, with retiring rooms, will be erected . . . All excursion trains before leaving town will be run to the Bennington Battle Monument. The grove, which is well watered and dark, with leafy shade in summer, is a popular resort, especially for Sunday ramblers, and is an admirable camping place for tourists. The locality is retired, and yet there is just enough dash of life in the vicinity to give piquancy and cheerfulness to a day's outing.

But celebrate as they would, there was still no battle monument. State legislation had been passed in 1853 (after Samuel Safford, the last local battle veteran, had died) and again in 1876 to incorporate a Bennington Battle Monument Association. Vermont promised $15,000 if another $5,000 could be raised by public solicitation; the states of New Hampshire and Massachusetts, whose patriots had played significant roles in the battle, were invited to contribute—but not, of course, New York, the territory of adversaries during the Hampshire Grants dispute. (The stone for the monument, nonetheless, eventually was quarried in New York State, at Sandy Hill, near the Hudson River.)

Hiland Hall was distressed when fund raising languished. Worse, disagreement arose over a concept for the battle monument's design. A prestigious design committee included the governors of Massachusetts and New Hampshire, plus Hall's friend E. J. Phelps, president of the American Bar Association, who would be President Cleveland's minister to Great Britain; along with Hall's grandson-in-law, John G. McCullough, a former attorney general of California, who was to become governor of Vermont in 1902.

This august group had studied monuments throughout the ages, including the Egyptian pyramids, Pompey's Pillar at Alexandria, the Nelson Monument in London's Trafalgar Square, and the twin towers of the new Brooklyn Bridge, which at 265 feet were then the tallest structures in all of New York. In December of 1884 the committee issued an erudite report that favored a story-telling or "artistic" approach. Members endorsed a model by Professor John W. Weir of Yale University for a monument 20 feet square

Above: architect J. Philipp Rinn, who drafted several monument possibilities before coming up with the winning design. Below: U.S. President Rutherford B. Hayes, who spoke at the monument cornerstone-laying rites in 1887.

17

Bennington has many attractions of current interest to the tourist and a wealth of historic sites and associations of which few towns can boast. There are no fewer than thirty-five spots that find a place in state or national history.

Thus will a visit to Bennington well repay the visitor in gaining knowledge of one of the most important events in American history as well as viewing the unsurpassed scenery from an imposing monument which commemorates the event.

—Bennington Banner, April 12, 1889

'Lookout' Tablets
Are Ready to Install

Preparations are being made to resume operations on the Bennington Battle Monument at an early date. Supt. A. G. Parsons is reported to have said that he hopes to complete the shaft this season. Architect Rinn was in town last week. Of the tablets proposed for the "lookout" room, only three societies are now sure, the F&AM, the I.O.O.F., and the [Vermont] Historical Society. Each stone will contain inscriptions and cost over $200.

—Bennington Banner, March 21, 1889

The view from the observation platform, two-thirds of the way up, looks out between stone slits upon a statue of Seth Warner, then on beyond—depending on the day's visibility—as far south as Mt. Greylock, the highest point in Massachusetts and recognizeable by its veterans' memorial tower.

Final Season of Work

The pleasant weather has induced Supt. Parsons to begin taking off the temporary roof of the Battle Monument today, and the laying of the masonry will soon commence. Should the season prove as promising as the opening there will be no doubt as to finishing the walls this season.

—Bennington Banner, April 4, 1889

Railway Promotes
Summer Tourism

The Bennington & Rutland railway has issued a handsomely illustrated and splendidly printed pamphlet of fifty pages entitled "Summer Homes among the Green Mountains," describing in language at once attractive and truthful the facilities which villages along the route afford the seekers after rest and recreation during the summer months. It is intended to bring the most beautiful and interesting region to the attention of tourists and summer residents.

—Bennington Banner, April 12, 1889

and 50 feet high, surrounded by four bronze allegorical statues each eight feet tall.

Hall was stunned. He sized up this proposal and harrumphed, "A little monument to a great event." It was he who had assembled the stellar committee that had come to this regrettable conclusion, and now he would have to disagree publicly with its report. "I cannot believe," he wrote, "that a monument to commemorate the important battle of Bennington, that is not of sufficient size and height to tower above its surroundings and to attract the attention and excite the admiration of the distant beholder, will command the approval of the public either of the three States that contribute to its erection or the people of the vicinity."

Although he was 89 years old, Hall undertook a public-relations blitz that would outmaneuver and overpower his own monument-design committee. In January 1885 a petition circulated in Bennington that cited "an honest difference of opinion" and asked the historical society to withhold a final decision. Hall's name headed the long list of signatories. He wrote letters to newspapers, gave public speeches, and in April organized a new distinguished design committee of no less than forty members to research the opinions of engineers, architects, and builders about the cost, durability, and stability of "a massive structure of commanding height." A smaller monument, he said in June, "would remain unknown to the world and would dwindle into an obscure art gallery."

In July, as he had hoped, the new advisory committee recommended an approach that would be "massive and lofty to comport with the mountains surrounding the site." The group

A portion of an old postcard that marks the site of General Stark's encampment the night before the battle; it is located on the Harrington Road and contains one version of the famous peptalk quote: "There are the Redcoats. And they are ours, or this night Molly Stark sleeps a widow."

Speaking Trumpet Needed

The monument is going skyward rapidly. It is now about 160 feet high, and the operators will soon need a speaking trumpet to give the directions to the men below.

—*Bennington Banner*, May 23, 1889

Rising Ten Feet a Week

The battle monument has now reached an altitude of 160 feet, almost ten feet a week. At this rate from fourteen to twenty weeks hence the capstone will be laid.

—*Bennington Banner*, May 24, 1889

Save the State Arms House

The building committee of the battle monument should use their best endeavors to retain intact the old State Arms House, a building that was erected the year the peace was declared and about the only remaining structure of Revolutionary times. It would answer a two-fold purpose, that of a memorial hall and a residence for the monument keeper.

—*Bennington Reformer*, August 16, 1889

Two-Ton Capstone Arrives

The Bennington Battle Monument stands 206 feet today. The capstone has arrived and will soon be cut into shape to lay. This stone weighs about two tons, and is heavier than either that of Bunker Hill or the Washington Monuments. The superintendent, A. Parsons, expects to put up the last thirty feet of the monument in fourteen days of good weather, and is confident he will finish the full 301 feet this fall as intended.

Work now is retarded somewhat waiting for stock. The G.A.R. tablet is in place, and is located on the south side of the lookout room. The Odd Fellows' will go in opposite; the Masonic tablet will occupy the east side, opposite that of the Historical Society on the west side.

Local members of the Masonic fraternity are not pleased with the workmanship of their tablet. Besides the other three, which are elaborate specimens of engraving and artistic skill, this tablet certainly shows to a great disadvantage. The

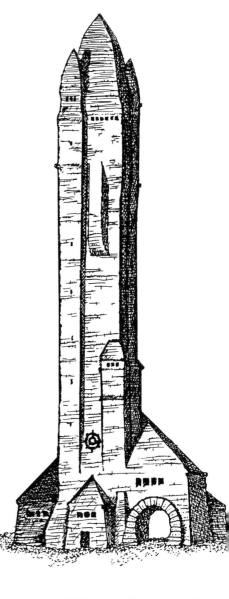

"Rinn's Big Tower," another rejected design, was the first suggestion for a 300-foot tower. It included a museum at the base, an idea abandoned for reasons of cost. A museum would not open for another forty years.

favored one of several designs by artist-architect J. Philipp Rinn of Boston for a mammoth granite shaft 301 feet high, tapering to a point from a base 37 feet square that would be anchored on bedrock. It was a satisfyingly far cry from Professor Weir's puny artistic proposal.

On Hall's 90th birthday, July 20, 1885, he was planning his strategy for the August 12 annual meeting of the Bennington Historical Society, when the final design decision was going to be made. The stage had been well prepared and Hall was not disappointed. By the time of the meeting, conducted by Vermont Governor Samuel E. Pingree, there was no argument. General McCullough himself moved to withdraw the Weir proposal. The approved design was Rinn's. Thus the new tower, Hall wrote:

. . . having its foundation on the brow of the high hill where stood the old revolutionary storehouse that General Burgoyne sought to capture . . . would be seen and admired for its beauty and grandeur by many thousand residents of the vicinity, and by a much greater number of travelers from abroad on the many miles of railroad that the monument would overlook. Such a monument I cannot

This stone marker, which few visitors see, on the lawn northeast of the monument, is dedicated to Anthony Haswell and to American press freedom. Vermont postmaster, printer, and editor of the Vermont Gazette, *Haswell chose prison to protest Alien and Sedition Laws, as did Vermont Congressman Matthew Lyon, re-elected while in jail for the offense. The laws were later overturned, Haswell posthumously pardoned; Lyon moved to Kentucky, was elected to Congress again from there. The stone marks the site of Haswell's home and print shop.*

ANTHONY HASWELL
1756 — 1816
EDITOR AND PUBLISHER THE VERMONT GAZETTE
BENNINGTON
UNCOMPROMISING IN DEFENSE OF FREEDOM OF THE PRESS
IMPRISONED IN 1800 FOR OPPOSITION TO ALIEN AND
SEDITION LAWS AS THREATS TO THE NEWBORN DEMOCRACY
ERECTED IN 1942
ON SITE OF FIRST PRINTING PRESS OF VERMONT GAZETTE BY
SIGMA DELTA CHI
NATIONAL PROFESSIONAL JOURNALISTIC FRATERNITY

designer of the combination emblem is greatly at fault, and the inscriptions are sadly marred by abbreviated words and ditto marks. It should never have been accepted, but it is now too late to mend matters.

—*Bennington Banner*, August 29, 1889

A Very Conspicuous Sentinel

The Bennington Battle Monument has reached the altitude of 220 feet and is still slowly rising upward to attain the allotted 301 feet. The correspondent of an exchange moralizes on our "pile of blue stones" after this fashion:

"The tall shaft, like a grim, gigantic sentinel guarding the valley of the Walloomsac, is a very conspicuous object in the landscape standing upon a commanding eminence, close to the site of the continental storehouse which Gen. Burgoyne sought to capture in Revolutionary times, it may be seen for many miles from almost any point of the compass. The top of the monument is now just 940 feet above the level of the sea, and the constant breezes and occasionally powerful winds which prevail at that height endanger the safety of the workmen engaged in laying the masonry of the structure, and so a heavy canvas wind-break has been placed around the top. No serious accident has as yet happened at the monument."

—*Bennington Banner*, September 26, 1889

'A Region of Charming Scenery and Pure Air'

Thirty-seven miles from Troy, and reached by four daily trains, making close connections with the Hudson River steamboats at Albany and Troy, and all trains East, South, and West, we find, nestled among the trees in the beautiful Walloomsac Valley, the village of Bennington, and looking down upon it from an elevation half a mile away, the old historic Bennington, now called Bennington Centre.

The charming Walloomsac River winds its way down to the Hudson through the centre of the village. Mt. Anthony on the west and Bald Mountain to the east, and a "panorama" of singular beauty. Northwestward, the Adirondacks, dim with the distance of a hundred miles; the Helderbergs and the Catskills to the south; Greylock, Saddle and Bald, and the long Green Mountain wall of

help but hope will in due time adorn our old State Arms Hill, though I cannot reasonably expect to live to see it.

Hall, a veteran of political wars in the halls of Congress as well as in the State House in Montpelier, had achieved his ultimate victory. His vision was uncannily accurate; the only difference is that today's visitors come by highway rather than by the railroads, which proved short-lived. As he also had foreseen, Hall did not live to see the monument. But at least when he died on December 20, 1885, he knew for certain that the "massive and lofty" obelisque would be built. It is a comfort to the rest of us that Hall's grave, in the burying ground of the Old First Church, marked by its own decorative Victorian column, is within sight of the battle monument he so ardently envisioned.

* * *

It took two years for the Bennington Battle Monument to rise to its full height against the skies near Mount Anthony. Funds came from state governments of Vermont, New Hampshire, and Massachusetts, the federal government, and from coins saved and donated by thousands of school children. In the spring of 1887 a $75,000 construction contract was signed. The state voted an extra $10,000 to acquire 10 parcels of land so the monument could be centered in a sizeable park. Unfortunately, that scheme required the demolition of the dignified brick State Arms House, where many Bennington Battle Day celebrations had been staged. Yet the plan assured a truly majestic setting for the new stone obelisque.

On August 16, 1887, the one hundred and tenth anniversary of the battle, the monument's five-ton cornerstone was dedicated with elaborate cere-

A steel engraving of President Benjamin Harrison, who gave two speeches in Bennington at the monument dedication (and Vermont centennial) in 1891. And his signature.

An important on-site marker is this marble designation of the location of the storehouse that was the objective of the British in Bennington —which they never reached. Stored here were horses, cattle, flour, corn, and other supplies badly needed by Burgoyne's army as it marched south from Canada. The marker is next to today's parking lot at the Bennington Battle Monument.

the east; Red Mountain, Equinox and Killington away to the north. And the just completed Bennington Battle Monument, a magnificent stone shaft which appears to pierce the sky as it rises 300 feet from the brow of the hill . . .

The delightfully smooth gravel roads, mountain trout fishing up streams which lead the charmed devotee of Izaak Walton far into the primeval forest.

Bennington Centre . . . with its main street so wide and so well adorned with grand old trees and well kept lawns as to constitute in itself a beautiful park, is one of the most charming country villages anywhere to be found, and is ever inch historic ground. The Walloomsac Hotel, 30 single, 10 double rooms, and rooms in dwellings near by. $10-$20 per week.

Healthy. Malaria, mosquitoes, and their kindred are here unknown; beautiful and historic.

Manchester, the principal summer resort of the Green Mountains. Equinox House, $17.50-$28 per week.

> —From *Summer Homes Among the Green Mountains*, published by the Bennington & Rutland Railway in 1889. [Note: "summer home" was used in the sense of a place in which one would spend an entire summer.]

VHS Presidents Memorialized

Among the expenditures of the past year is the item of $225 for a memorial tablet for the Bennington Battle Monument. The tablet is of Barre granite, 5 feet and 9 inches long, 3 feet and 3 inches wide and 2 inches thick. It bears the seal and motto of the Vermont Historical Society cut in bas relief, has the following inscriptions carved upon its face: "Vermont Historical Society, organized 1838, Presidents: Henry Stevens, Hiland Hall, George F. Houghton, Wm. H. Lord, E. P. Walton." (From a report of an annual meeting of the VHS at Montpelier on October 15.)

> —*Bennington Banner*, October 24, 1889

Removal of Scaffolding
Discloses a Work of Art

The scaffolding is coming down rapidly from the Bennington Battle Monument, and the beautiful proportions of that structure, now seen to be a work of art, become more and more ap-

monies that attracted 30,000 people to town. Documents and memorabilia, including the late Hiland Hall's Early History of Vermont, filled a cavity under the stone, and scores of members of the Masonic Order performed their rituals to seal the premises for all time. Throughout 1888 the structure gradually grew taller by means of a temporary rail line, scaffolding, and a steam-powered hoist.

In November 1889, as the monument's capstone was hauled up and cemented into place, another grand ceremony was held. Thirty dignitaries rode up the crude scaffold elevator and took turns standing for a few dizzying moments at the very top, waving to a crowd of about 3,000 that included many descendants of battle veterans. The event was covered by newspapers from Bennington, Rutland, Burlington, Troy, Boston, and New York. The Bennington Banner reported dramatically that when the ceremony ended ". . . the sun burst forth from the cold clouds, and the first sunset upon the Bennington Monument was one of splendor."

Even more extravagant ceremonies took place in August 1891 when the monument's formal dedication was combined with the centennial of Vermont's admission to the Union as the fourteenth state. A parade of 4,484 persons (by actual count) and 511 carriages and saddle horses marched through Bennington, and a banquet was served to 5,000 under an outsized tent. President Benjamin Harrison made two speeches, and there were many other orations, prayers and sermons, accounts of the battle, histories of the state, and "postprandial ceremonies."

Among those who traveled to Bennington to see the president of the

parent as the disfiguration is removed. This is the highest battle monument in the world and stands on a site 283 feet above the Walloomsac River. The structure itself is 301 feet 10½ inches from the bottom of the cornerstone to the top of the capstone, and 307 feet 9½ inches to the top of the star. Bennington has not only the highest battle monument but the highest single-jet fountain on the globe.

—*Bennington Banner*, December 26, 1889 (The fountain referred to was that in front of the Vermont Soldiers' Home.)

The Mighty Shaft That Commemorates Bennington's Heroes and Their Victory— How the Monument has Climbed Upward— And Now the Capstone is to be Set— The Event and Its Perpetuation in Stone.

The Bennington battle-monument has almost ceased to climb further into cloudland. In a day or two the capstone, which weighs nearly two tons, will be lifted to its dizzy resting-place, and the tall shafts will be crowned with a star. The exterior of the monument will then be finished.

THE SECOND HIGHEST

It will be the second highest structure of the kind on the continent, for it will require a line 308 feet long to reach from the top of the foundation to the tip of the star.

A DOUBLE MEMORIAL

Many years ago the people of Bennington conceived the idea of erecting a suitable memorial to those who fought and fell in the battle, and at the same time making it serve to commemorate an important event in American history, for nearly all historians now concede the importance of the battle of Bennington in securing the independence of the colonists.

In 1853 the necessary legislation was secured for forming an association for the erection of a monument, but the project fell through, mainly from lack of influence and funds.

A SOCIETY FORMED

But the cherished idea of building a monument was not abandoned, though action was held in abeyance until 1875, when the Bennington historical society was formed, with the object of

A grand ceremonial arch, made of canvas painted to resemble granite, spanned Bennington's Main Street in August 1891 to glorify the massive double celebration: centennial of Vermont statehood and dedication of the massive and lofty new 300-foot Bennington Battle Monument. In the crowd, utterly obscure, was 19-year-old Calvin Coolidge of Plymouth, Vt., who came to see the president of the United States, and who would become president himself during an August ceremony 32 years later.

United States was one Calvin Coolidge of Plymouth, Vt., then 19 years old. He wrote later, "As I looked on him [Harrison] and realized that he personally represented the glory and dignity of the United States I wondered how it felt to bear so much responsibility and little thought I should ever know."

Now August 16 is Bennington Battle Day, an annual Vermont state holiday when (on the Sunday closest to that date) Bennington's volunteer firemen stage a big parade to commemorate the battle. Hiland Hall and J. Philipp Rinn would surely be pleased to know that their monument has weathered its first century and is still amply appreciated. Visitors and residents alike have reason to applaud the hard-fought design decision of 1885 that selected the "monumental" concept over the "artistic" and brought them the renowned landmark which the monument has become.

The imposing statue of Seth Warner, whose regiment clinched victory at the Battle of Bennington, was dedicated in 1911, a gift of Bennington industrialist Olin Scott. The photo was taken in 1987 before a small steel balcony was attached to monument's uppermost portal.

not only putting up a battle-monument but of also marking all the historic sites of the town. So the monument is really the child of the historical society. The influence of a large number of prominent men over a wide section of the country was enlisted in the matter, and in the course of two or three years the enterprise began to take on form and dignity.

HELP FROM STATES AND CITIZENS

The states of Massachusetts, New Hampshire and Vermont and the general government were appealed to for aid, as each of these states had troops in the battle. Nearly all the money that was solicited from these sources was promptly given. An appeal was also made to a large number of wealthy men, many of whom were former residents of Vermont, throughout the country, and the sums realized in this way have largely swelled the monument fund.

CHOOSING BETWEEN TWO DESIGNS

When about $100,000 had been secured the matter of a design came up, and it was very generally agreed that the monument should not be distinctly sculptured, but be an architectural affair, of lofty and massive yet simple proportions. The Weir design called for a monument abounding in sculpture, having a heroic figure at each corner, and the structure was not to exceed sixty-six feet in height. Such a monument was deemed proper for a city square, but not for rugged scenery, deep valleys, high hills and bold mountains. The Weir design had some strong advocates in the association, however, but mainly through the exertions of ex-Gov. Hiland Hall the Rinn design, which called for a simple shaft more than 300 feet high, was almost unanimously adopted by the association.

—Troy, N.Y., *Times*, November 23, 1889

CROWNING A MONUMENT.
Capping Bennington's Historical Shaft
The Waving Flag at a Dizzy Height—
The Shouts of the Spectators—
Next will be the Dedication.

Yesterday at sunrise three heavy guns boomed through the valley at Bennington, and shortly afterward the American flag was seen floating from the top of the Bennington battle-monument. The

For fifty years the local Bennington Monument Association operated the battle monument, hired a caretaker and groundskeeper and charged a modest fee—originally ten cents—to visitors. In the early days a person would first pick up the key at the caretaker's home, use it to open the great bronze doors, then climb in near darkness up 417 graceful iron steps to the observatory at the 188-foot level for the reward of gazing at distant countryside through vertical stone slits. Especially in pre-aviation times, it was a rare vista. To the south one could see practically the entire village of Old Bennington, where the prisoners and wounded from the battle had been brought for safekeeping on that great day in history. On a clear day the view stretched all the way south to the highest point in Massachusetts, Mt. Greylock, where a war-memorial tower, erected in 1932, is today visible. To the west and north, one could look out the monument's clefts and envision the route General Stark and Seth Warner and their victorious patriots took upon returning from the battle. And to the east, the vista encompassed a great expanse of the Green Mountain range along with the growing industrial and residential village of Bennington.

In the 1940s the association discovered that its monument needed expensive repairs. Trustees of Old Bennington

The cannon nick-named "Molly Stark," one of four captured from the British at the Battle of Bennington, as depicted in an early postcard. One cannon is in the Bennington Museum, another on the steps of the Vermont Statehouse in Montpelier.

day had come to lay the capstone of the towering shaft. The sky was overcast with gray clouds, a strong breeze prevailed and it was decidedly cold and unpleasant in the open air.

THE CAPSTONE.

A little past 2 o'clock about 15,000 persons had gathered to witness the laying of the capstone, which was suspended from two wire cables on the south side of the monument, and which was partly covered by a Masonic flag and a beautiful bouquet.

THE ASCENT.

At precisely 2:45 o'clock, amid the discharge of cannon, the signal was given to set the engine in motion, and the huge stone was slowly lifted to the place of honor, 301 feet high, on the monument, the ascent occupying just six minutes.

A GREAT SHOUT.

As the stone was lowered and placed in position a great shout went up from a thousand throats, and the boom of cannon told the story to all the people for miles around.

A WEIGHTY STONE.

The stone, which is pyramidal in form, is three feet and four inches square at the lower surface, and tapers to eight inches square on the upper surface. It is said to weight several hundred pounds more than that of the Washington monument. The capstone was fastened by a bolt having a ball for its head, and surmounted by a ten-pointed star, all of gun metal and weighing 300 pounds.

THE FLAG OF MASONRY.

Finally a beautiful Masonic flag, 24×36 inches, the gift of Superintendent Parsons, was flung to the breeze from the dizzy summit of the completed monument. The flag, which was of blue silk, trimmed with silver and having on its field an embroidered square and compasses with the letter "G.," will be presented to Mount Anthony Lodge, F. and A.M., as the cornerstone was laid by that ancient fraternity on the anniversary of the battle, August 16, 1887.

FROM NOW TILL THE DEDICATION.

An iron stairway will be put in, several dwellings removed and four acres of land properly graded before the monument will be dedicated, an event that will not occur until August 16, 1891.

—*Bennington Banner*, November 25, 1889

This grandiose "artistic" concept of a monument design would have incorporated statues of battle heroes from Massachusetts, New Hampshire, and Vermont.

Village expressed fears about liability if someone were injured by a falling stone. By 1953 the association notified the governor that it intended to disband, no longer financially able to maintain the structure. Rumors even spread that the obelisque might have to be razed.

The state of Vermont, which already owned the site, came to history's rescue, placed the monument under jurisdiction of its Board of Historic Sites, and soon made needed repairs—notably with exterior repointing. Windows were fitted into the lookout slits, and the graceful square metal staircase, modeled after the Farnese Palace in Rome (said to have been designed by Michaelangelo) was closed to the public both for reasons of deteriorating metal supports and because of vandalism and graffiti. An elevator was constructed inside the stairway, and that became the lone means of reaching the observatory. The view suffered slightly because the windows prevented a visitor from thrusting one's head too far out between the narrow stones. Now the view was potentially distant, depending on the day's visibility, but not panoramic. Because of the stone's thickness, one could—and can—see north, south, east, and west, but only one direction at a time.

A highlight in the monument's history was the time a Vermont governor personally climbed to its capstone, an effort not to be taken lightly because it involves ascending a slightly backward-leaning ladder in virtual darkness from above the 200-foot lookout level up to a tiny door near the pinnacle. The task requires a steely fearlessness of heights. This accomplishment was that of Governor Robert T. Stafford of Rutland, who later served for many years as a U.S. senator and is

BENNINGTON BATTLE
Finishing the Monument—
An Imposing Structure—
Interesting Incidents.

The work which W. H. Ward of Lowell, Mass., contracted to do in erecting the Bennington battle monument will be completed in two or three days. The masons for a number of weeks have been engaged in finishing the cementing of the interior of the structure and in putting in substantial stone floors.

The lightning rod runs down the inside of the monument and leads to the bottom of a well thirty-four feet deep. A great deal of work, however, remains to be done. A stairway is to be put in, but it is not yet decided whether it will be of wood or iron. The monument association has sufficient funds to put in a wooden stairway, but a bill is before Congress and has passed the Senate for money to build an iron stairway. The association will probably wait a while to ascertain the fate of the bill.

A number of acres of land will have to be properly leveled and graded and several houses removed before the monument will be dedicated. The expense of this undertaking, however, will be borne by the state of Vermont. When all obstructions to the view have been removed, the great memorial shaft will stand out in bold relief—simple, graceful, grand. Seemingly it is a perfect success as a work of art. It pleases the eye and produces an agreeable feeling that leads one to look long and frequently at its charming curve-lines, which constantly change the direction of the outline, but so gradually that it is difficult to determine their beginning or end.

As originally suggested by Prof. Truman Bartlett, the well-known Boston artist, the right angle corners of the shaft where the sides meet, and also at all windows and other openings, the stone is finished in half-inch draft lines or arris; that is, it is finished smoothly and along these lines the stone is pitched off and brought on line with joints of ashlar, so that arris and joint come to one plane. This device adds much to the artistic beauty of the shaft. It breaks what otherwise might be a hardness of lines at the corners and helps to give the column an airiness and gracefulness that constitute one of its most agreeable qualities. The sharp-

Another "monument" to the Burgoyne campaign is Fort Ticonderoga, the key to Lake Champlain, which the British recaptured in 1777 on their way south. Back in 1775 the fort was captured from the British by Ethan Allen in one of the first and most dramatic events of the American Revolution. Today the historic site attracts nearly 100,000 visitors a year.

now retired. For this writer, Stafford recalled that he made the climb, probably in 1961, to settle an argument.

"A rather acrimonious debate" had developed, he said, between two state officials, each known for a degree of curmudgeonry, over the quality of the repointing of the monument's upper portion. Vrest Orton of Weston, then chairman of the state Historic Sites Commission, understood that the job was done poorly, and Perry Merrill, commissioner of forests and parks, thought it was just fine.

There was a technical reason for the disagreement, and that involved the precise proportions of sand, water, and cement used in the mortar. Too much cement and the action of freezing and thawing could actually split the monument's stones; too little and the mix might not hold.

Governor Stafford, not wishing to see two such prominent personages engaged in a public quarrel, decided to inspect the work himself. He had learned in the Navy to be nimble on ladders, and so he climbed up and out the uppermost hatch near the summit,

ness of outline is in no way diminished by this arrangement, while it gives an added ease to the whole structure and what might be termed a graceful movement, for the eye is carried thereby involuntarily from the base to the apex even when the finished line itself has disappeared, melting away imperceptably as the height increases.

FROM THE EAST

All the fine qualities of the monument are seen to the best advantage when looking at it from the east, just as the sun has sunk behind the high western hills and the sky is thickly streaked with bright lines of radiance. The flaming background brings out the wonderful symmetry of the shaft and gives it a poise and gracefulness that has never been surpassed in any other structure of equal massiveness and height.

OTHER FEATURES

Prof. Bartlett recommended the entasis of the structure, and it is the first application of it in a modern monument. The elongated top is a creation of Prof. Olin L. Warner, the sculptor. Nearly all the other points of the structure were designed by Prof. J. Ph. Rinn of New York. The view from the upper landing is grand and impressive. On one hand lies the teeming valley of the Walloomsac, with the shining river rolling to the sea. Bold hills rise on every hand, crowned with patches of old and sturdy trees or vast sweeps of forest, and far-off mountain ranges, outlining their desolate peaks on the sky, fill out a perspective in which the grand is seldom more strikingly pictured.

OBSERVATIONS OF STRANGERS

A large proportion of the strangers who go to Bennington visit the monument. Sometimes a surprising amount of ignorance is exhibited by them in historical matters. For instance, one gentleman wanted to know if the battle of Bennington was fought during the revolution or during the war of the rebellion. Another had never heard of Gen. Stark, the immortal hero of the battle. But one lady, a member of a traveling theatrical troupe, has borne off the palm for ignorance of the true purpose of the monument. She supposed the structure was simply a huge gravestone, erected to mark the resting-places of those who fell in battle. The actress was showily dressed, and her brass jewelry would have sufficed for the ransom of an African

Not until the battle's bicentennial in 1977 was there a site marker at Bennington honoring the role of General Stark. On August 16 that year this rock, with much bronze verbiage, was placed near the monument entrance, by the N.H. American Revolution Bicentennial Commission. The text reads: "Erected in honor of Brigadier General John Stark and the 1,400 New Hampshire men who came to the defense of Vermont in August 1777. Assembling at Fort Number Four in Charlestown, N.H., Stark and his troops crossed the Green Mountains to aid in the defense of the newly established state of Vermont as the commander-in-chief of all the

(continued on page 36)

then up to the peak by means of a short exterior ladder that was shaped somewhat like a tube, but beneath which there was nothing but 300 feet of air. Stafford was accompanied by Clayton Buxton, state sergeant-at-arms, and closely followed by a Bennington Banner reporter armed with a 4-by-5 Speed Graphic camera, big and clumsy by today's standards.

"When we returned to the ground," Stafford reminisced, "we advised Mr. Merrill and Mr. Orton that the monument had been properly repointed and invited either who wished to doubt it to climb the monument to see for himself. Neither decided to do so but elected to take Mr. Buxton's and my word for it."

"That ended the dispute," Stafford concluded, "and my only regret is that the Banner reporter who wrote a story on the matter—as he himself said in some anguish in his story— had no film in his camera that morning."

As a tourist attraction, this gargantuan paperweight covers only its immediate expenses, though it is visited by about 50,000 persons a year, a number larger than any other site maintained by the state Division of Historic Sites.

The structure requires long-term maintenance on a scale as grand as its height. Excess humidity from condensation on cold stone pervades the interior and gradually deteriorates steel beams and the old iron stairs, ultimately affecting the masonry. Various remedies have been tried, including an oil-heating system— abandoned during the energy crunch of the 1970s—and ventilation. Fortunately there is no steel framework to deteriorate because the monument is built solely of stone, at least two layers of it, and is thus self-

The Seth Warner statue appears from this angle to stand as a sentinel to guard Mt. Anthony, in the distance.

king. Tipping her head back until it rested on her shoulder blades, she slowly surveyed the 308 feet of masonry, from the foundation to the tip of the star, and then closely examined the ground around the shaft. "Why, I don't notice any graves about here. Were the soldiers buried under that tall thing?" said she, pointing a three-ringed finger to the monument. Some of her companions "audibly" smiled at the simplicity of the remark, and the color of the lady's face quickly assumed the hue of an over-ripe tomato.

  —Troy, N.Y., *Daily Times*, May 5, 1890

Workman Miraculously Survives 200-Foot Interior Plunge Into Monument's Basement

  On November 30, 1888, construction on the Monument had ceased for the season. That morning Frank Nolan and Tom Stewart, two young men regularly employed on the job, were sent to the top to begin construction of a temporary roof for winter protection. They were drawn up by a hoisting engine located on the ground. By the same means lumber was drawn up for their use.

  The accident seems to have been due to misunderstandings and misinterpretation of signals too complicated to be unraveled at this late day.

  Suffice it to say Mr. Nolan lost control of himself at the top of the second year's construction and fell to the basement on the inside of the Monument. His fall was broken every ten feet by a succession of inch boards through which he broke. It might be more proper to say his whole descent was made up of a series of ten-foot falls.

  Mr. Stewart followed his friend and co-worker as soon as possible and was prepared for the worst. To his great surprise and relief he found Nolan not only conscious but seemingly not much impaired. To avoid chances, Mr. Nolan was carefully placed upon a stretcher and taken to his home where a physician failed to find anything wrong.

  That same evening, as no bones had protruded, friends calling found him up around the house. After an incredibly short time he was back on the job. His only physical reminder of his experience was a very slight scalp wound where hair refused to grow.

  The writer was in the village that day. It was reported on the street that Frank Nolan had fallen

(continued from page 34)

American forces from New Hampshire, Vermont, Massachusetts and New York. General Stark had approximately 2,000 men in all in the first phase of the battle. General Stark's army defeated and captured a British detachment led by Lt. Col. Friedrich Baum. Shortly after this triumph with the timely assistance of Col. Seth Warner and his 'Green Mountain Boys,' a relief column under Col. Heinrich von Breymann was repulsed. By thus denying the enemy sorely needed supplies, these twin victories near Bennington on August 16, 1777, contributed notably to the total British surrender at Saratoga two months later and to the subsequent military alliance with France, the turning point in the war for American independence. Presented to the state of Vermont by the New Hampshire American Revolution Bicentennial Commission."

supporting. It budges not the least in a windstorm.

In the early 1990s the monument was again scaffolded while another expensive round of repointing was completed on the exterior masonry, and a small steel balcony was placed beneath a new ladder that leads from the uppermost door to the very summit. It is safe to say that the century-old monument will indeed be around for several ages to come, and so long as the proper proportions have been mixed in the cement, the stones should hold together for many more years.

This Victorian monument to Hiland Hall, whose arguments prevailed for a "Massive and lofty" Bennington Battle Monument, is now in the burying ground of the Old First Church, within sight of the monument itself. Hall's grave itself is marked by one of the stones in the foreground.

one hundred and sixty feet and lived to tell the tale. Mr. Nolan was reluctant to discuss the accident but is known to have said when pressed for a definite answer that his fall started at the outlook windows. The windows are two hundred feet above the ground and the basement is somewhat below the surface.

In later life Frank Nolan for many years delivered mail on the streets of Bennington. Tom Stewart founded the Stewart Grocery on lower River Street now conducted by his daughter and her husband, Mr. and Mrs. Herbert F. Dumas and "Stu."

> —As reported by Lee F. Armstrong
> in the *Bennington Banner*'s
> "Ginger's Travel Talk" column
> April 18, 1949.

Must Fight Its Own Battles:
The Wind and the Monument

Our Bennington, Vt., correspondent writes:

Exaggerated newspaper reports have led many to believe that the heavy windblows in April, or defective masonry or water percolating through the masonry and subsequently freezing, have materially injured the Bennington battle-monument. The facts are that a dozen stones, possibly more, of the tall shaft are fractured. These fractures are fine and threadlike, and would be passed by unnoticed in most cases unless a person were looking for defects. The corner-stone is fractured in two places, one on the south and one on the east side, but the janitor is positive that he discovered these breaks two or three years ago. None of the stones is crushed or split, as each block of dolomite is laid parallel with the cleavage of the stone, thus preventing any accident of that kind. So far as has been observed all the fractured stones are within twelve or fifteen feet of the ground, the majority being below the first six or seven courses of masonry.

Apparently the stability of the structure is not affected by the damage, so far as it has been discovered. The interior of the monument is uninjured, though the iron staircase is getting rusty in spots and needs repainting. The outlook at the grand landing is unprotected by windows or doors, and it is thought by some that heavy rains have been driven under the floor, which is intended to act as a roof, and that the water has percolated through the masonry and in freezing has caused all the mischief. Some of the fractures are moist and in one in particular water stands in drops, thus giving some color to the theory that the action of frost last winter was the cause of the damage.

A large number of visitors, mostly from surrounding towns, registered at the monument yesterday. A stiff breeze from the west prevailed, however, making it disagreeable and even dangerous to stand on the upper landing. The wind at that height raised its voice at times and wailed aloud. The grand views in the warm green valley below, the sunlight on the hills and the tumult of mountain peaks in the distance were more pleasantly seen from terra firma than from the high and giddy shaft.

—Troy, N.Y., *Times*, May 23, 1893

A Triumphal Arch Will Span Main Street

Probably the culminating feature of the work of the Committee on Decorations will be the triumphal arch which will span Main Street at the intersection of North and South streets. The structure, which will be covered with cloth and painted and striped so as to resemble the Bennington battle monument stone, will be fifty-two feet long and the extreme height forty-seven feet, surmounted by a living Goddess of Liberty. There will be a number of elaborate balconies and platforms, with banners, mottoes, emblems and numerous artistic decorations. The coat-of-arms of the United States and Vermont will also be used.

Some has proposed to call it the "living arch" as 100 female singers and a large number of prominent people will occupy the structure when the procession passes under it. The mottoes and many of the details of the decoration have not been determined on. It is thought both sides of the arch will be brilliant and very attractive.

Work was commenced Monday on this structure and the framework is already well along. Will C. Bull, chairman of the committee, is the designer and builder.

—*Bennington Banner*, July 17, 1891

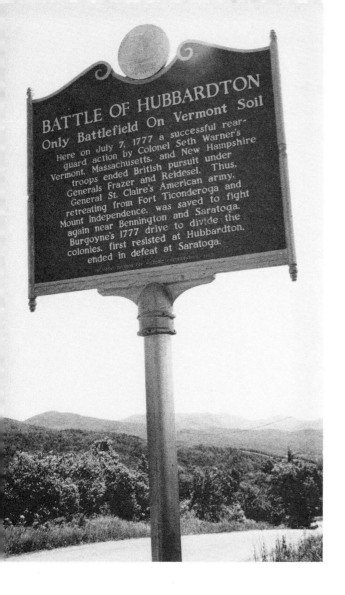

BATTLE OF HUBBARDTON
Only Battlefield On Vermont Soil

Here on July 7, 1777 a successful rear-guard action by Colonel Seth Warner's troops ended British pursuit under Vermont, Massachusetts, and New Hampshire Generals Frazer and Reidesel. Thus, General St. Claire's American army, retreating from Fort Ticonderoga and Mount Independence, was saved to fight again near Bennington and Saratoga. Burgoyne's 1777 drive to divide the colonies, first resisted at Hubbardton, ended in defeat at Saratoga.

Hubbardton Battle Monument
The only battle ever fought on Vermont soil, an early event in the Burgoyne campaign, has been commemorated since 1859 by this handsome marble marker at Hubbardton, near Castleton. Like the Bennington Monument, it is administered by the Vermont Division of Historic Preservation

40

Saratoga Battle Monument

This 155-foot memorial to the victorious turning point of the American Revolution stands on a hillside in Schuylerville, N.Y. A few miles away, an interpretive center operated by the National Park Service is available to visitors. Saratoga's monument, unlike Bennington's, was dedicated on the centennial of the battle in 1877; as the closeup shows, its design is far more decorative, more "Victorian," than Bennington's.

An optical illusion photo, above, in conjunction with the Old First Church: sometimes you see the monument, through the tree branches, sometimes you don't. And a 1905 postcard view of the broader scene.

A yen for touching the Monument's star
(or: how do they change the light bulb up there?)

A closeup view of the monument's light bulb fixture, 300 feet in the air. If one bulb quits, the other one comes on.

I remember the night it struck me. Frigid and crystal clear under a January moon, the red beacon atop the Monument shone with exceptional intensity. During the previous twenty-three years I had driven past Bennington's famous obelisque hundreds of times and never made the connection. The lamp on the pinnacle must house a bulb. The bulb must fail periodically. Ergo someone must **change** the bulb.

Warm spring weather and the opening of the Monument's visitor's center rekindled my desire to find out who maintained the light at the top of Vermont's tallest structure. Different shades of curiosity motivated me. On the one hand, I wanted to meet the person who got paid to clamber about places better suited to crows than human beings. More importantly, I wanted to be there myself.

At the time (it was April 1988), Shelley Hight served as the monument's caretaker. Since most questions

Text and photographs by Julius Rosenwald

43

The rolling topography of Mt. Anthony, a 2,300-foot Taconic mountain, as seen from the monument's capstone, more than 1,100 feet above sea level.

she fielded centered on the Battle of Bennington, history of the area, and the construction of the edifice itself, my inquiry took her aback. "The bulb," she laughed. "You want to go with Jill when she changes the bulb? The one at the top?" With no small hint of disbelief at my request, she gave me a phone number and said, "Give her a call and see what she says."

Jill Mason's responsibility for bulb servicing went back to 1985 but she knew the routine long before that. "I work for Charlie Pray [a tree surgeon in Bennington]," Jill explained. "He changed the bulb for as long as I can remember. I'd always go with him so I could yell to the caretaker, who was turning the switches down below, to make sure the new lights both worked. There are two up there—the main and a backup. A few years ago Charlie gave the Monument job to me."

Rather than wait for trouble, Mason changed the bulbs twice a year. "Forget trying to do it when it's ten below and windy. I try to get up there in late October and then again in April or May. We shoot for a day with no wind and no rain.''

After a round of if-it's-okay-with-her-it's-okay-with-me between Hight and Mason, we chose a day for the ascent and hoped the weather cooperated.

I will never forget that day. Like a child on Christmas morning, waiting anxiously to go downstairs and behold unopened treasures, I felt the butterflies in my stomach growing and multiplying by the minute. Out the door, point-and-shoot camera and notebook in hand, the adventure had commenced.

Driving down the avenue into Old Bennington, past the First Church and the elegant houses, the stately maples draped in their first spring foliage, the Monument seemed more majestic than ever. It also seemed taller than ever. From below, the iron ladder leading to the capstone's star looked like a dollhouse miniature. My palms felt damp.

Standing on the lawn at the base of the Monument, gawking to see the top, it felt surreal to anticipate the radical change in perspective whereby

The photographer's shoe, closeup and in sharp focus, lends perspective from the very top of the monument, looking down 300 feet at the monument's gift shop.

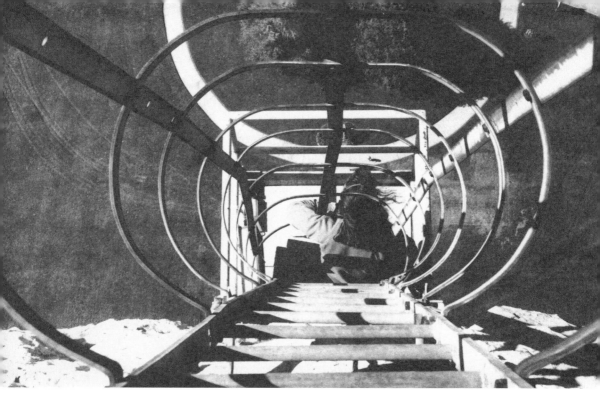

Gazing down upon the monument's upper balcony through its protected upper ladder.

I would soon be looking straight **down** 305 feet. Hight ushered Mason and me into the elevator with the reassuring words, "This is the easy part." Few lifts that ascend twenty stories can boast such a simple button-selection panel. No sub-basements, mezzanines, or penthouse. Just up, or down. Every year tens of thousands of tourists take this whirring ride to the observation deck at the two-hundred-foot level and peer through vertical windows at the surrounding countryside. Mason and I had considerably further to go.

"From here on it's closed to the public," she smiled and opened a curved metal door in the northeast corner of the observation room. We climbed a single flight of circular stairs and entered an eerie darkness. We stood on the platform that supports the elevator's motor and counterbalance mechanism.

Craning my neck, looking up at the eight-story iron ladder disappearing into the half-light of the Monument's inner sanctum, I dismissed questioning the prudence of this adventure.

Some explanation is required to understand the photograph below. It was taken by holding the camera over the very tip of the capstone, shooting down the east face of the monument. The tiny object on the ground is the Anthony Haswell marker that commemorates American press freedom. In foreground is one of several pitons or spikes built into the monument's masonry from which scaffolding may be hung.

Before going up herself (only one person on the ladder at a time!), Mason had checked my saftey harness and a contraption that clipped onto a metal strip. Any downward pressure would cause the device to clamp and lock, thereby preventing a fall. She then dashed my momentary sense of security by saying, "The only problem with this thing is it gets caught at the joints on the way up and you have to let go with one hand to unstick it. See you there!" Off she went.

Because the Monument tapers to a point, the ladder does not follow the contour of the wall but stands in mid-air, held in place by steel brackets set into the mortar. I tried to tell myself they did **not** look tenuous as the sound of creaking iron reverberated with every vertical footstep Mason took. It seemed interminable, watching her slowly vanish up into dimness. At last I heard her open the trap door at the top and shout, "Okay. You can go."

Putting my left foot on the first rung, clenching the fourth run in my right fist, I ventured upwards toward the pinnacle. I'd scaled many ladders

over the years but never one that did not lean in against a wall. With each handhold my fingers felt like vises, clutching with the force of a pit bull's jaws.

I imagined The Little Engine That Could and methodically moved up to my goal. At last Mason's voice sounded close by. "You're almost there." Through the trap door and I'd made it. We stood on a small floor inside the peak of the Monument.

"Now all I have to do is take out this metal shutter and we can go outside." Mason spoke with the calm tone of someone about to open a screen door to the porch. She removed a louvered panel thereby exposing a two-foot-square opening. "You go ahead. It's easiest to slide your feet through first," she said.

Slithering through the hole, I gained access to a tiny platform suspended from the Monument's exterior west facade. Shelley Hight stood on the lawn below and waved. She looked like a gnat. The scale of her caretaker's house resembled a building in a model railroad layout.

Mason poked her head out. "Go on up. You can see 360 degrees from the capstone." A final external ladder led to the peak. Another fifteen feet and I arrived. Face to face with the bronze star, its ten points much larger than expected, I peered around the corner and saw them: two lights in red glass housings. These beacons had led me to a truly magical spot.

Five years passed and some things changed. Mary Lou Chicote became the Monument's caretaker. Jill Mason no longer looked after the bulbs. And funds finally became available to point up the structure's masonry.

For me, the allure of the capstone had not changed. When I heard that my friend Tyler Resch wanted current

While photographs were being taken from the capstone, 301 feet 10.5 inches in the air, the photographer was being observed from below by more than a handful of monument visitors. Barely visible inside the tiny steel balcony, about twenty feet below the capstone, is monument caretaker Mary Lou Chicote. The statue of Seth Warner at left seems to add to the occasion's drama.

photographs taken from that vantage for a book about the Bennington Monument, I quickly volunteered my services.

Chicote seemed enthusiastic about the project and we selected a day for the ascent that coincided with the brilliance of autumn foliage. Parking at the Monument on that October morning, I did not feel the same jitters as "the first time." Still, the eight-story iron ladder commanded a healthy respect in my memory.

The procedure Chicote and I followed didn't differ from the original: the elevator, the long ladder climb, the trap door. Only when I slid through the opening onto the platform and stood face-to-face with Mount Anthony did I have a jolt of reality.

While my challenge five years before had simply involved accompanying Jill Mason, now I had pictures to take, with a non-automatic camera. The logistics of focusing, selecting apertures and framing shots assumed a heightened tension given a somewhat precarious stance three hundred feet off the deck. Safety remained a paramount concern, and to that end I'd worn a rock-climbing harness and secured it to the capstone with a length of nylon webbing.

The sun, the clarity of the air, and hillsides of gold and scarlet combined to make for one of those dream-like moments we want to capture and keep in all its intensity, stored intact forever. Nothing could compare. Peering out the window of a small plane might give a hint of the view from the capstone. Drifting over Bennington in a hot-air balloon might come closer.

Yet I had the luxury, the privilege—without moving—of simply looking. The Adirondacks to the northwest, the Catskills to their south, Mount Equinox and the emerald meadows of

Shaftsbury to the north. Photographing the landscape to the east proved a bit more harrowing, and I managed to snap a shot straight down the east face of the Monument by simply aiming the camera from the capstone.

Clinging to the capstone while putting the forests of Glastenbury in the camera's viewfinder, I thought about the men who placed this pyramid-shaped stone here more than one hundred years ago. For a moment I shared a sense of wonder with the few lucky enough to have touched the Monument's star.

The Battle Monument

Proud shaft, that riseth through the sky
   To greet that second heaven
Of glory, where men never die
   Whose lives for men were given—
Thy lesson worketh in our souls
   Belike a fiery leaven.

No man may look upon thee long,
   Thy mighty mass admiring,
Without dividing right from wrong
   And unto right aspiring;
A moral eloquence is thine
   Which speaks in tones untiring.

Proud shaft, great teacher, solemn pile,
   Whose praises let no lip shun,
Thy lines commemorate the Nile,
   Thy form is half Egyptian,
Yet on thy facets not one glyph
   Image or superscription.

Thy seat commands the shot-torn Hill
   Where Patriots strove for Freedom;
A place today for daffodil
   And sunny banks of sedum;
The Hill wherefrom no man turned back
   As Israel did at Edom.

Proud shaft, that riseth near the spot
   Whereto, with zeal elated,
The Fathers brought from close and cot
   The stores their hands created—
The stores a sullen king would seize
   Whilst trembling subjects waited.

Thy height o'erlooks the sacred place,
   Where housed from wind and weather,
First gathered those, who, touched by Grace,
   Were glad of heart to gather;
Where many a wounded dragoon died
   And Tory felt the tether.

Proud shaft, the deep historian's line
   Is weak beside they teaching;
The spirit of that day 'tis thine
   To make far-read and reaching;
Arouse us that we act our parts
   Beyond a world's impeaching.

One of several poems written by Daniel L. Cady for the celebration in
1927 of the 150th anniversary of the Battle of Bennington.

Bennington Battle Monument Facts

Why, When, Who

* Origin: Erected by Bennington Battle Monument Association, incorporated by Vermont legislature November 18, 1876, to construct suitable monument to commemorate Battle of Bennington, August 16, 1777. Battle itself, 5 miles away in Walloomsac, N.Y., can be said to have leveraged American independence because it led to British surrender after Battles of Saratoga, September and October 1777, regarded as turning point of American Revolution.

* Timeframe: Cornerstone laid August 16, 1887; capstone cemented November 25, 1889; formal dedication held August 19, 1891. (Dedication coincided with 100th anniversary of Vermont's admission to Union as 14th state after 14 years as independent republic.)

* Location: Marks site of storehouse that was objective of British General John Burgoyne, heading from Canada for Albany with large army which needed food and horses; other Brits aimed for Albany from south and west; none made it.

* Operation: Since 1953, owned and operated by state of Vermont's Division for Historic Preservation.

Building Blocks

* Construction: All stone on stone; no framework.

* Exterior: Sandy Hill dolomite, quarried near Hudson Falls, N.Y., a blue-gray magnesian limestone with reputation for hardness and durability, hauled here by rail on temporary tracks.

* Interior: Stone mostly from local quarries.

* Foundation: Rests on limestone excavated down to bedrock, between fifteen and twenty feet.

* Decor: At 168-foot level, exterior rough stone surface changes to smooth horizontal beltcourse 8 feet high, above which a series of 20 vertical, 11-foot slotted openings provides observation lookouts. Above that is another beltcourse 13 feet high.

* Solidity: Monument does not sway even in high wind.

Statistics

* Measurement at base: 37 by 37 feet square, tapering to pyramid-shaped capstone.

* Capstone: 4-foot-4 square at base, 3 feet high, 8 inches square at top, supporting 10-pointed bronze star that serves as lightning rod point.

* Weight of capstone: 2 tons.

* Weight of bronze star: 125 pounds.

* Thickness of walls: 9 feet at bedrock foundation, 7-foot-6 at ground level, 2 feet at apex.

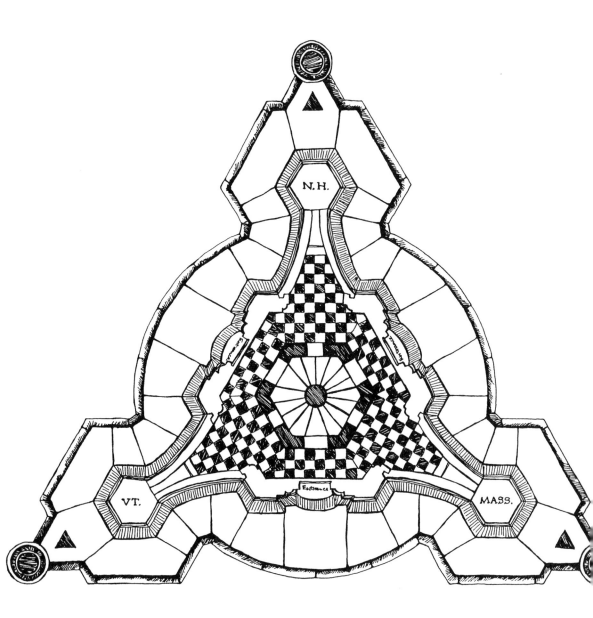

On exhibit in the Bennington Museum is the original architect's drawing—
from which this sketch was made by artist Karen Kane—of R. M. Chambers's
proposal for a triangular artistic monument to the Battle of Bennington.
Elements of the triangle were to represent militia units from the partici-
pating states of Vermont, New Hampshire, and Massachusetts, and their
respective heroes, Seth Warner, John Stark, and Parson Thomas Allen.

* Height from base of cornerstone to top of capstone: 301 feet, 10½ inches.

* Height from base of cornerstone to top of star: 306 feet, 4½ inches.

* Cornerstone: Best guess: southeast. (Cornerstone, in which 19th-century documents and memorabilia were placed and sealed ceremonially by members of Masonic Grand Lodge in 1887, is unmarked and no one is certain any more which corner it really was.)

* Number of visitors: Averages 50,000 a year; total in 1992: 46,617; largest number in recent years: 54,000 in 1987. Site attracts more than any operated by state of Vermont.

Interior

* Entrance hall: 20 feet square, 39 feet high, contains granite tablets dedicated to participating states of Vermont, New Hampshire, and Massachusetts. Beneath: Cellar 10 feet high.

* Observatory room: 18 feet square, contains commemorative tablets (above windows) of Barre granite: north, Vermont Historical Society; east, Grand Masonic Lodge; south, Grand Army of Republic; and west, Independent Order of Odd Fellows.

* Access to observatory: By elevator only; originally by rectangular iron staircase modeled after Farnese Palace in Rome, said to have been designed by Michaelangelo. Number of flights of stairs from entrance to observatory: 34; number of steps: 417. Stairway, subject to rusting, closed to public for safety reasons since elevator was installed by Vermont Historic Sites Commission, which took ownership and restored monument in 1953.

* Relic that has hung inside monument's entrance ever since 1891 dedication: Camp kettle captured from forces of surrendered British General John Burgoyne after Saratoga.

* Subject of diorama inside entrance: Second of two engagements of three-hour Battle of Bennington.

Historical

* Cost of monument and site preparation: $112,000, paid through private subscriptions, federal appropriations, plus states of Vermont, New Hampshire, Massachusetts, which sent patriots to battle.

* First contribution toward a monument to Battle of Bennington: $100 given February 10, 1876, by Mrs. Ominda Gerry, 88, known as "Aunt Ominda," reputed for parsimoniousness. Her father, Hopestill Armstrong, had fought in battle.

* Principal orator dedicating monument in 1891: Edward J. Phelps, former U.S. minister to Great Britain, president of American Bar Association, member of original monument design committee. Also speaking, among many dignitaries: U.S. President Benjamin Harrison.

* Principal architect of monument: J. Philipp Rinn of Boston.

Et Cetera

* Feature of original design agreed upon in 1887 and not yet carried out: Bas relief sculptures of heads of battle heroes from three states: Seth Warner from Vermont, Parson Thomas Allen from Massachusetts, General John Stark from New Hampshire.

* Statue south of monument: Seth Warner, whose regiment was credited with clinching victory; dedicated in 1911, gift of Bennington industrialist Olin Scott.

* Statue of General John Stark, military leader of victorious forces at Bennington: None exists at this site (but a commemorative boulder in his honor was placed near monument entrance by New Hampshire American Revolution Bicentennial Commission in 1977).

* Location of remains of allies and adversaries who fell in battle: Common gravestone in burying ground of Old First Church, a block south.

* Another "Bennington Battle Monument": A smaller granite obelisque memorializing battle is located north of village of Peru, Vermont, in northern Bennington County, on site where Stark's 1,000 men reportedly camped on route from Charlestown, New Hampshire.

* Bennington vs. Saratoga: Bennington's monument is nearly twice as tall as 155-foot Saratoga Battle Monument, located on hill at Victory Mills, Schuylerville,N.Y. Saratoga Monument cornerstone was laid in 1877, centennial of battle, with completion in 1883; whereas Bennington cornerstone waited until 1887, completion in 1889, dedication in 1891.

* Other historic sites operated by state of Vermont: Calvin Coolidge Birthplace at Plymouth, Senator Justin Smith Morrill Home at Strafford, Old Constitution House at Windsor, Eureka Schoolhouse at Springfield, President Chester A. Arthur Birthplace at Fairfield, Hyde Log Cabin at Grand Isle, Hubbardton Battlefield at Hubbardton, Mount Independence at Orwell and Chimney Point near Addison.

* Other sites in Vermont relating to Burgoyne campaign of 1777: Hubbardton Battlefield, Mount Independence.

* Interpretive sites in New York State relating to Burgoyne campaign: Fort Ticonderoga, Saratoga National Historical Park, Saratoga Battle Monument, Bennington Battlefield State Park in Walloomsac.

56

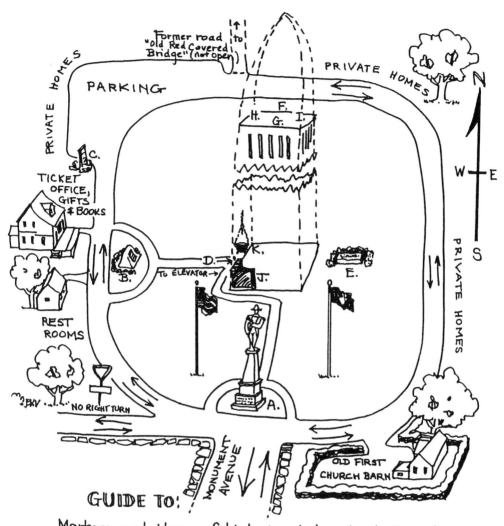

GUIDE TO:

Markers and items of historic interest at the site of

THE BENNINGTON BATTLE MONUMENT
(elevator to 200 foot observation deck)

A. Seth Warner Statue–Placed in 1911. Warner's victorious role amply described in inscriptions at base

B. John Stark commemorative stone–Placed in 1977. Role of New Hampshire Militia described in bronze text on stone.

C. Site of Continental Storehouse (corn, flour, horses, cattle) which was the objective of the British attack.

D. U.S. Geodetic Survey benchmark embedded in monument to the left of entrance showing elevation of 873' above sea level.

E. Marker to Anthony Haswell, press champion, on site of his house and print shop.

F. Inscription in granite (look above north window in observatory) to Vermont Historical Society founders, including Hiland Hall

G. "   "   " (above south window) to Grand Army of the Republic.

H. "   "   " (above west window) to Independent Order of Odd Fellows

I. "   "   " (above east window) to Grand Masonic Lodge

J. Diorama of the Battle of Bennington scene.

K. Kettle for cooking, captured from the British at the battle.